FAMILY WALKS AROUND THE BLACKWATER VALLEY

CONTE

To My Darling Shân
With All My Love

Published by
FOOTMARK PUBLICATIONS
12 The Bourne, Fleet, Hampshire

Adrian
xxx
x x
x

FAMILY WALKS SERIES

Family walks around the Blackwater Valley 2000. ISBN 0 9527363 5 7
Family Walks around Hook, Hartley Wintney & Rotherwick 1999
Family Walks around Odiham & Upton Grey 1998
Family Walks around Fleet & Crookham 1997

Great care has been taken to be accurate. The publisher cannot however accept any responsibility for errors which may occur, or their consequences. All walk descriptions have been checked independently, but changes can occur. **If obstructions or crops on the line of the path are encountered, please contact the Rights of Way Officer asking for the problem to be cleared. Give a map reference if possible.** Address and telephone numbers are:

Rights of Way Officer, (Hampshire)
Basing House,
Basing,
Redbridge Lane,
Basingstoke RG24 OHB
Tel: 01256 29663

Rights of Way Officer, (Berkshire)
PO Box 153,
Shute End,
Wokingham,
Berkshire RG40 1WL
Tel 0118 974 6991

ABBREVIATIONS

R	Right	SP	Signpost
RHS	Right hand side	S	Stile
L	Left	FB	Footbridge
LHS	Left hand side	W	Waymark

INTRODUCTION

This book covers twelve circular walks around the Blackwater Valley, and includes some from *Family Walks around Eversley & Yateley* that has been out of print for a few years. The walks straddle the Hampshire - Berkshire border with a slight excursion into Surrey. The popular format of the walk description and its accompanying map on facing pages is retained. Points of Interest seen from the walks are described separately at the end of the book.

The paragraph numbers in the walks correspond to the numbers shown on the maps. Starting points for the walks (where parking should be available) are shown on the map in the centre pages. However walks can be started from any point provided the circular direction is followed. Bus services run to some of the local villages covered by the walks.

Ordnance Survey *Explorer Maps* 145 & 159 at a scale of 2½ miles to the inch shows all the paths in detail and walkers are encouraged to use these maps although those in this book are adequate.

The walks pass close to public houses where refreshments are available for thirsty walkers. Please ask the landlord for his permission if you wish to leave your car in the car park. In dry conditions good walking shoes should suffice, but wellies may be needed in wetter conditions.

Dog owners please keep your dog on a lead where livestock are present and it is probably wisest to avoid fields with livestock and their young.

Some walks pass close to private houses — please respect the residents privacy.

My thanks to Ted Blackman for the sketch maps (based on out of copyright maps and path surveys) and to the following for checking the new walks: June & Mark Beckley, David & Jane Eccles, Tony & Marianne Morgan, Myrtle & Annette, Ted & Bridget Payne, Pat Sansom and Steve & Pam Turner.

Bob Rose
Fleet, April 2000

12·3·06

Walk No 1　HEATH WARREN & LOWER COMMON

Stopped nite uour in

[4½ miles, 2¼ hours]

1. Start from Eversley Church. Go through the churchyard and leave it by a gate at the rear. Follow the enclosed footpath, cross a footbridge and through a kissing gate to go along the LH field edge. In the field corner, cross a foot-bridge, through a kissing gate and ahead along an enclosed path. Go through two further kissing gates and along a track at the edge of a wood. At the end of a field on your R, cross a track and continue ahead (ignoring side turnings) on the track. After 700 yards, just before overhead pylon wires, at a 4-fingered signpost on your L, turn R on a path through trees and grass passing a gas depot on your R to reach and cross a road with care.

1A. Note. To visit Cudbury Clump, turn L at the above mentioned 4-fingered signpost and follow a path through a new plantation and some tall pines to join the Welsh Drive. Cudbury Clump is the low mound on your L by the bridleway signpost.

2. Enter Bramshill Plantation (car park on your L). At the signpost, go ahead on the footpath under the pylon wires. In ½ mile look out for and go through a kissing gate on your R and along an enclosed path. Leave the path by a kiss-ing gate and turn L along a shingle drive to reach a road.

3. Turn L along New Mill Lane and after passing Rycroft look out for a metal footpath signpost on your R. Turn R along the enclosed path, through a kiss-ing gate, turn R across two paddocks to a kissing gate by a signpost. Turn R along an enclosed path and shortly cross a footbridge. Turn L at a 2-fingered signpost, do not enter the field, but follow the path through holly bushes. Go over a stile and turn L at kissing gate to reach another kissing gate in the field corner. Turn R across a meadow, through a kissing gate and along an enclosed path to reach a road.

4. Turn R along The Street; watch traffic, keep on the RH footway. Pass the White Hart and shortly after the turning to Warbrook House at the end of the wooden barrier, turn R at footpath signpost and along a path through woods. Pass the football ground on your L and in due course reach the road by The Lodge.

5. Cross the road carefully and take the shingle drive to the L of Longreach. Keep ahead on the drive to Lyndridge . When the drive bears R, go through a kissing gate and along an enclosed path. Turn L through a kissing gate, over a footbridge and along the RH field edge to return to Eversley Church.

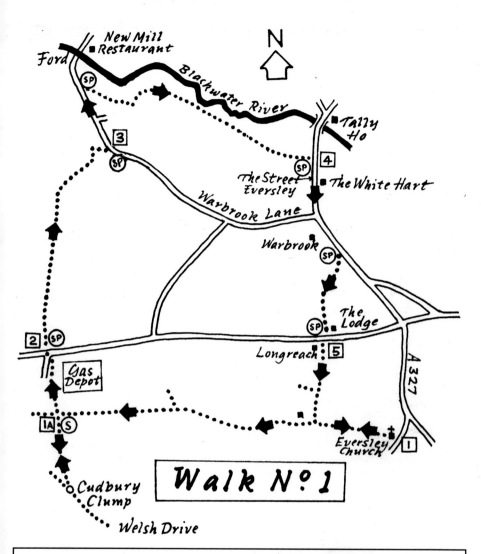

New Mill Restaurant
Ford
Blackwater River
N
Tally Ho
3
The Street Eversley
4
The White Hart
Warbrook Lane
Warbrook
2
Gas Depot
The Lodge
Longreach
5
A 327
1A S
Eversley Church
1
Cudbury Clump
Welsh Drive

Walk Nº 1

Walk No 2   WELSH DRIVE & CASTLE BOTTOM

[5 miles, 2½ hours]

1. Start from Eversley Church. Go along Church Lane, at some white gates, turn L at a footpath signpost up a track through the woods. At the top of the hill, bear L at a waymark post along a parallel track and at another waymark post, fork L on a track leading to a SAGA pillar in an open space. Turn L along a wide gravel track (the Welsh Drive) to reach and carefully cross a road to a bridleway signpost opposite. Continue on the Welsh Drive to cross carefully Coopers Hill.

2. Go through the gap and immediately turn L on the marked bridleway. At a T-junction, turn L on the bridleway and then R (following a large earth bank on your R). Do not take the first stile on your L, but continue ahead and turn L over the next stile by a gate. Follow the earth track and at a crossing track, turn R on a path that in due course descends on steps and crosses a stream [Castle Bottom on your R]. Continue on the path up some steps to cross a stile by a gate.

3. Turn L along a stoney track (with a wooden paling fence on your L). The track narrows, forks L then R and shortly reaches and crosses an open space. Turn L on a path descending through holly trees to cross a footbridge. Cross the field diagonally to a wooden gate in its opposite corner, continue half L across the next field to the L of a house and paddock and through a kissing gate in the field corner.

4. Turn R along the road [passing Firgrove Manor on your L]; at the T-junction, cross the road carefully , through a gap in the trees and turn L on a path running parallel to the road. In due course keep along the road on its RHS - beware traffic. At the cross roads, go ahead on Up Green and at the T-junction turn R along Chequers Lane. [Keep along Chequers Lane to visit pubs]

5. Shortly turn L at a metal footpath signpost along a tarmac drive, over a stile and along an enclosed path with woods on your L. At a crossing track, keep along the path on the LH field edge. At the wood corner, turn L along an enclosed path by a green gate with the field on your R. Ignore a footbridge on your L, but at the field corner, cross a footbridge and stile to enter a field. Follow the hedge on your L and shortly at waymark post, turn L along the LH field edge to cross a stile in the field corner. Turn R along the RH edge of two fields, over another stile and a kissing gate. With great care, cross the road and return to Eversley Church.

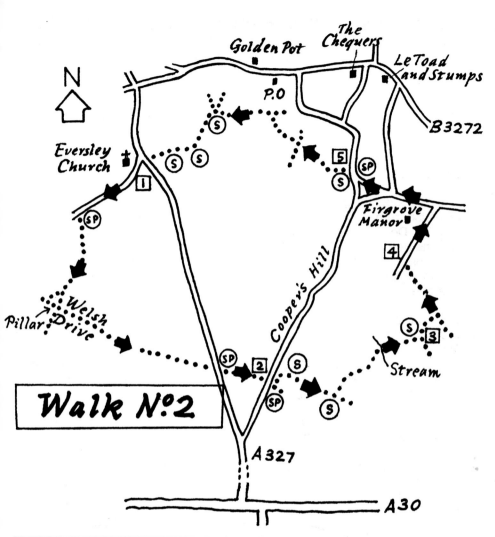

N

Golden Pot

The Chequers

Le Toad and Stumps

B3272

P.O

Eversley Church

Firgrove Manor

Cooper's Hill

Welsh Drive

Pillar

Stream

Walk Nº2

A327

A30

Golden Pot
Eversley

Good range of cask conditioned ale

Interesting bar food menu available 7 days a week lunch and evening

Separate a la carte restaurant

Swiss rosti night every Monday night

Traditional Sunday lunch served from 12 noon

Telephone: 0118 9732104

Justin, Antoinette and the Team look forward to welcoming you

Walk No 3   EVERSLEY CROSS & UP GREEN

[4 miles, 2 hours]

1. Start from Eversley Church. Go down the track away from the church and with great care cross the road to the metal footpath signpost about 30 yards to the R. Go through the kissing gate and along the LH field edge, cross a stile and at the corner of the second field, turn L over a stile and along the RH edge of a large field. At a waymark post, turn R along a hedge, cross a stile in the corner of a field, over a footbridge and along an enclosed path. At the end of this path (by a green gate on your L), leave the woods on your R and keep ahead on a track; shortly bear left on a footpath across the field (soon with a wire fence on your R). Go through a kissing gate to reach Hollybush Lane.

2. Turn R along the lane; at the T-junction turn L along Chequers Lane. [Keep along Chequers Lane to visit pubs] About 70 yards beyond a white house on your R, turn R at a footpath signpost, over a stile and along an enclosed path to reach the B 3272.

3. Cross this road with great care and go along Fox Lane opposite. Just beyond Fox Cottages on your L, turn L at a footpath signpost, over a stile and along an enclosed path; continue ahead through gravel workings and over a stile . Turn R and shortly L at a waymarked post and go between trees. In 50 yards turn R along the RH field edge and over a stile in the field corner. Follow the enclosed tarmac path, forking R and turn R along Crosby Gardens to the B 3272.

4. Cross this road with great care (using the traffic island) to a byway signpost opposite. Go along this track to pass Firgrove Farm Cottage on your L. Just before the byway signpost, turn R on a path running parallel to Firgrove Road. In due course this path merges with the road - beware traffic. At the cross roads, go ahead on Up Green. At the T-junction, turn L along Up Green (turn R along Chequers Lane for pubs) and just beyond Up Green Farm, look out for a footpath signpost on your R by a gate.

5. Turn R over a stile and along an enclosed path with the farm on your R. Cross two adjacent stiles and a track and follow the RH field edge to a foot-bridge and stile in the field corner. Turn R and then L along a track (with woods on your R). At a farm gate, take the LH of two stiles and go diagonally half-L across a field to a stile in its LH corner. Go over the next stile just opposite and along the LH field edge, cross a stile in the field corner and then two foot-bridges with a pond on your R. Go under a electrified wire protected by blue hose, along the LH field edges, under another protected wire and head for the field corner. Go through a gate, turn L on a marked footpath by farm buildings and along the drive to the road. Turn R along the RHS of this road - beware

traffic, take extreme care! When it is safe, turn L across the road and return to Eversley Church.

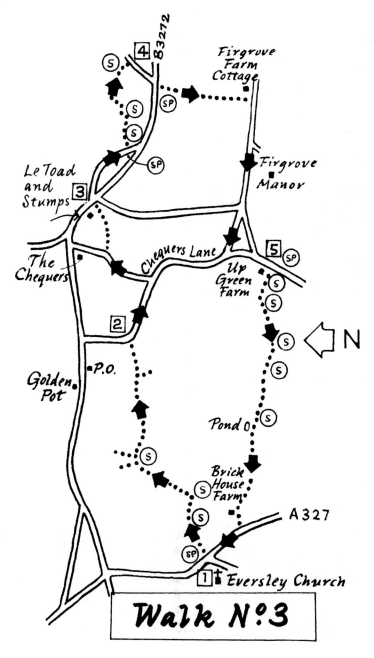

B3272

4

S

Firgrove
Farm
Cottage

S

SP

S

SP

Le Toad
and
Stumps

3

Firgrove
Manor

The
Chequers

Chequers Lane

5 SP

Up
Green
Farm

S

S

2

S

⟵N

P.O.

S

Golden
Pot

Pond o S

S

Brick
House
Farm

S

A327

S

SP

1 ✠ Eversley Church

Walk Nº3

Walk No 4   YATELEY COMMON COUNTRY PARK

[3½ miles, 1¾ hours]

1. Start from the Royal Oak, Yateley. Go up Royal Oak Close, turn L past the Police Station, up steps and turn R along the Royal Oak Valley Footpath with a wooden fence on your L. Cross a track and continue on an enclosed path with a wooden fence on your R (crossing a further track). At an open space, cross a track and continue ahead on the path passing The Cricketers on your R. Keep ahead on the LH path through the trees and at a bridleway signpost, turn L along Handford Lane to Cricket Hill Lane.

2. Cross the road carefully, turn R and shortly at BT phone box, turn L along track to Yateley Common Country Park. Shortly at a T-junction, fork L up the track (car park on your R) and go across the grass to the path on the edge of Wyndhams Pool. Turn R on this path and follow it round the pool end, go up the path through trees. Shortly turn hard R on another path and ignoring all side turnings , keep ahead. Go up two steps, cross a track and a further track in oak trees. The path gradually bear L and runs close to the A 30. Ignore all side turnings and in due course pass a wooden pylon. The path shortly descends some wide steps and in about 80 yards on bears L with the fields on your L to arrive at Strouds Pond.

3. Turn L at the T-junction and pass Strouds Pond on your R; continue ahead on the track and pass Cottage Farm on your L. Turn L at the T-junction, do not enter the farm gate, but take the narrow path through some trees with fields on either side (can be muddy). At T-junction, turn R along a wide track to pass Heathlands Cemetery. Continue along the road, turn L at the T-junction down Stevens Hill to Cricket Hill Lane.

4. Cross the road carefully to Beaver Lane opposite, fork R at The Triangle, then fork L passing Twangate Cottage. In about 40 yards,turn R along a narrow path (with a wooden fence on your R) and return to the Royal Oak.

N

Walk Nº 4

Royal Oak

The Cricketers

Handford Lane

Wyndham's Pool

Heathlands Cemetery

Cottage Farm

Stroud's Pool

Cricket Hill Lane

Ely

A30

Walk No 5   LONGWATER & FINCHAMPSTED CHURCH

[4 miles, 2 hours]

1. Start from the Tally Ho*, by the Blackwater River, Eversley. Turn R up Fleet Hill - beware of traffic; in 250 yards at Vann House, turn R at a footpath signpost along a lane, marked the Blackwater Valley Footpath. Pass some paddocks and farm buildings on your R, cross two stiles by farm gates and go along the track on the LH field edge (with Fleet Copse on your L). At the farm gate, cross the stile and keep to the LH field edge. At the end of the long field, cross a stile and turn L at a footpath signpost along the path that joins a road. [Note the Catherine of Aragon plaque on your L on a footpath signpost]

2. Keep ahead on Longwater Lane through houses; at the T-junction, turn L along the road [go ahead for The Greyhound] and R at the next T-junction. In 50 yards, cross the road with care to a footpath signpost opposite. Go up the enclosed stoney track/path passing the cricket ground on your L. Keep up the hill passing a seat on your R, ignore the LH turning at a footpath signpost, go ahead through the kissing gate and into churchyard.

3. Leave the churchyard by the RH gate, descend a few yards at a footpath signpost and turn L along Church Lane passing a red brick house on your L. Descend on the track, forking R at Manor Beacon on an enclosed track. Go through a kissing gate and cross the private drive to a kissing gate opposite and follow the enclosed track between fields. At a 4-fingered footpath signpost, go through the posts to an enclosed path on the RH field edge with a wire fence on your L. Pass a wood on your R, continue on an enclosed path, cross a stile and a minor road to a kissing gate opposite by a footpath signpost.

4. Cross the field with a wire fence on your R to another kissing gate. Turn R along the road keeping on the RHS (watch the traffic) and return to The Tally Ho.

Please ask the Landlords permission to park.

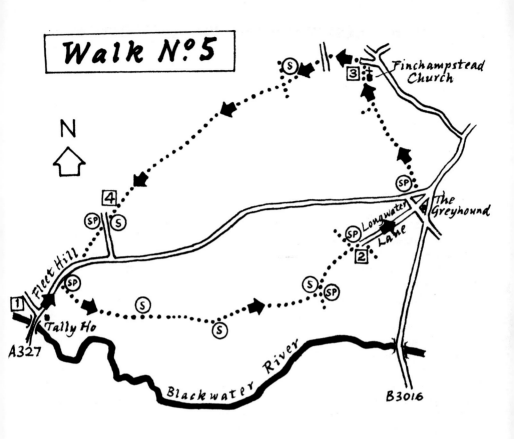

Walk Nº5

Finchampstead Church

N

Fleet Hill

A327

Tally Ho

Blackwater River

Longwater Lane

The Greyhound

B3016

The Tally Ho

Telephone: Eversley 01189 732134

The Tally Ho welcomes you to a traditional village pub

Real Ale & Good Food available
Lunch and Evenings
Large Garden

Walk No 6 FINCHAMPSTEAD RIDGES & MOOR GREEN LAKES

[4 miles, 2 hours]

1. Start from the Horseshoe Lake car park. Go along the track to the Watersports Centre and turn R along the lakeside path. Go through three kissing gates, cross the road with care to the footpath signpost and kissing gate opposite. Keep along the LH field edges, over a stile and through the final kissing gate to the road. [Turn R to visit Ambarrow Court or start from there]

2. Turn L along the road; at Bluebells Farm sign on your R, turn R at the footpath signpost and go along the track. At the Y-junction, fork R on the path with fields on your L and a wood on your R. Fork R at a waymarked post and ascend through the trees. At a T-junction, turn R at a bridleway signpost along the track and shortly turn L at a footpath signpost and along a track passing a white building on your L, continue ahead to reach Wellingtonia Avenue. [Look R to see the giant Sequoia trees lining the Avenue]

3. By the NO PARKING sign, bear L on a permissive footpath and go across the heath. Shortly turn L at a waymarked post and descend through the woods [keep ahead at the waymarked post to visit Finchampstead Ridges viewpoint]. At a large fallen tree on your L, turn L on the path by a waymarked post [passing a NT *No Horses Beyond This Point* notice on your R] along a winding path leading to a bar gate. [Spout Pond is a few yards along the path to your R] Go through the gap by the bar gate and turn R at a bridleway signpost along the track descending to the road at Moor Green House.

4. Turn R along the road; in 300 yards opposite Pithers Cottage, turn L at the footpath and bridleway signposts along the enclosed Blackwater Valley Footpath. [The walk can be started from the car park here] At the Blackwater River, turn L along the riverside path. Do not cross the footbridge over the river, but continue along the riverside. At the HORSESHOE LAKE sign, go through the kissing gate and continue along the riverside path eventually arriving at but not joining Mill Lane. Turn L at the footpath map along a gravel path and over duckboards along the waymarked lakeside path to return to the car park and the walk start.

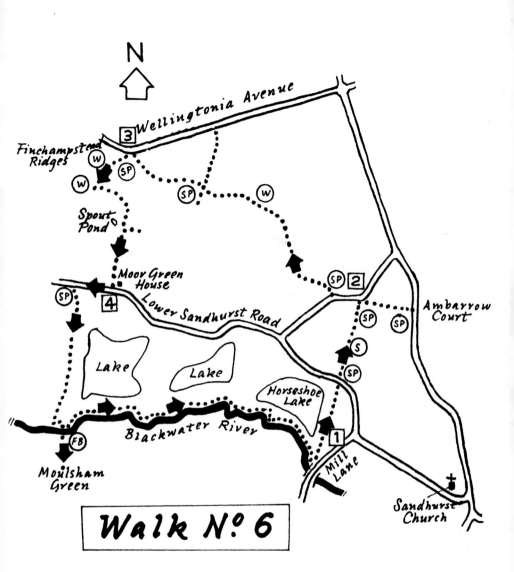

N

Wellingtonia Avenue

3

Finchampstead Ridges

W W SP

SP

W

Spout Pond

Moor Green House

Lower Sandhurst Road

SP

4

SP 2

Ambarrow Court

SP SP

S

SP

Lake

Lake

Horseshoe Lake

Blackwater River

FB

Moulsham Green

Mill Lane

1

Sandhurst Church

Walk Nº 6

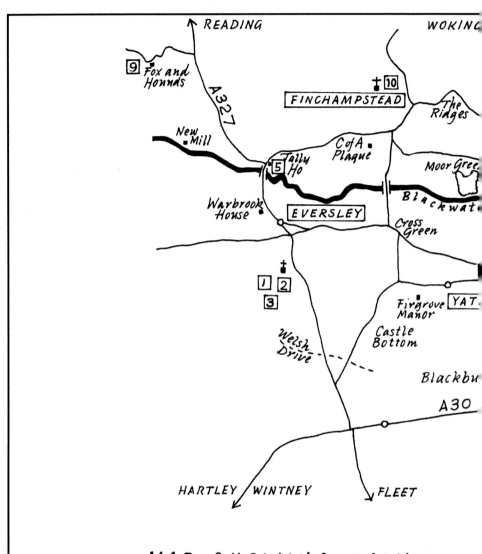

MAP SHOWING WALK
STARTS 1 - 12
AND POINTS OF INTEREST

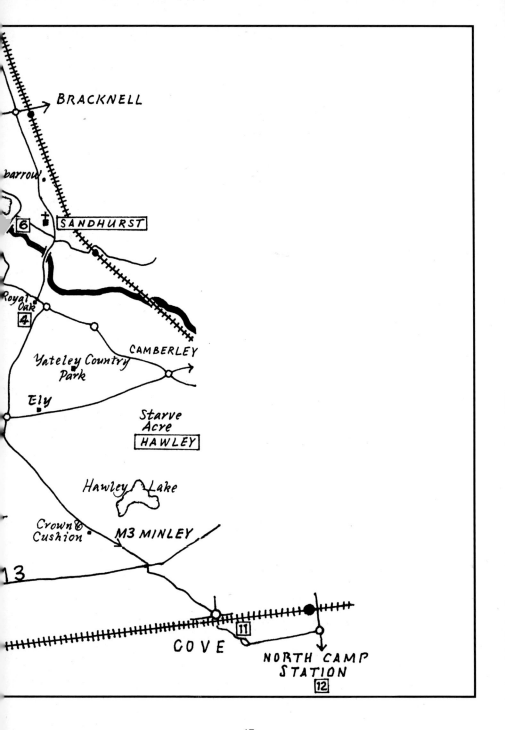

BRACKNELL

barrow

6 SANDHURST

Royal
Oak
4

CAMBERLEY

Yateley Country
Park

Ely

Starve
Acre
HAWLEY

Hawley Lake

Crown
Cushion

M3 MINLEY

3

COVE

11

NORTH CAMP
STATION
12

Walk No 7 YATELEY GREEN & BLACKBUSHE

[4 miles - 2 hours]

1. Start from Yateley Town Council Offices. Go along the B 3272 Reading Road and turn L at The Link; at the T-junction, turn L and shortly fork L on the path across Yateley Green. Cross Hall Lane and follow the footway passing the White Lion on your L and the Dog & Partridge on your R. Go through St Peters churchyard on a tarmac path to the L of the church. Leave the churchyard and go ahead for 150 yards, turn L along a path that passes beside school playing fields.

2. Cross a road and go along the bridleway opposite. Shortly pass, but do not take the path on your L that leads to the Royal Oak pub. In 50 yards at a small concrete post on your R, turn R along an enclosed path. At a crossing drive-way, keep straight ahead passing The Cricketers and Yateley Baptist Church on your R. Ignore the L fork, but keep ahead on the track through the trees to reach Handford Lane.

3. Cross the road to a bridleway opposite and follow the track marked 'Residents Access Only' passing some houses on your R. Continue past Oakhaven straight ahead until the end of the houses, take the track at the bridleway signpost through the woods. Shortly after passing under power cables, turn R along the crossing track uphill soon crossing an old road. Keep ahead on the path passing a Gas Pipeline post (can be muddy). Reach the road by the junction with Dungells Lane.

4. Cross the road diagonally R and follow the track opposite leading to a gravel track. Ignore all side turnings, just before an earth bank, turn R on a track through gorse bushes and turn R again along an old tarmac track then go over a bank to a road. Turn L along the road (extreme care with traffic) to the Anchor Inn on your R.

5. Turn L up Little Vigo and soon turn R. At the end of the houses, cross the track and in 25 yards turn R to reach an open grass area. Turn L on a path that crosses old airfield hard standings. Keep ahead and at the end of an old run-way, fork R through gorse bushes. At the end of houses on your R, turn R at old oil drums along a gravel track. At a T-junction, turn R and immediately L along Monteagle Lane.

6. Pass the Poets Corner pub and continue ahead on Old Monteagle Lane with the school playing fields on your R. Cross School Lane and bear L on a foot-way and cycleway. At Waitrose, turn R along Monteagle Lane. At the round-about, bear R and cross Firgrove Road, go through the wooden barrier oppo-site and along the enclosed path. After 200 yards, fork R at a wooden seat and

go through two wooden barriers. At a concrete bollard, go on the path through some trees which leads to a large open grass area and The Link. Turn L and then R to return to the start.

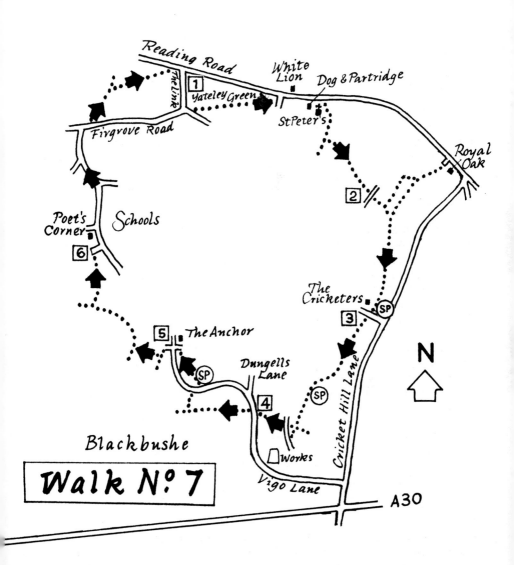

Walk No 8   MINLEY & HAWLEY LAKE

[4 miles, 2 hours]

1. Start from the junction of Minley Road (A 327) and the B 3013 . Enter the Defence Lands via a stile by an EMERGENCY ACCESS NOTICE. Go ahead on a broad track, after 500 yards at an ARMED PATROLS notice, ao not bear L but keep ahead on a track by jumps. Ignore crossing tracks, descend, cross a road and go ahead. Shortly fork R on a track through trees with fields on your L. In due course cross a concrete road (by large white pyramid bollards), short-ly bear L on a track (bridge on your R). At a Y-junction, keep ahead on the track. Just beyond some overhead pylon cables, meet a crossing bridleway.

2. Turn L at the waymark post along the bridleway. In 500 yards, at a waymark arrow on a post, turn L and shortly R along the bridleway. Keep ahead ignor-ing side turnings; in due course pass a wooden gate and along a short length of tarmac road.

3. Cross with care the busy A 327 Minley Road to a bridleway signpost oppo-site. Go ahead on an earth track through trees, turn L at a waymark post along a track. Pass a metal barrier, turn R along the tarmac road. Pass the Royal Engineers training area and Hawley Lake. Just beyond the Sailing Club the road narrows, pass a metal gate and in 200 yards LOOK OUT for a crossing track and waymark post, turn L along the gravel bridleway that becomes sandy. Turn L at a crossing track and in 40 yards turn R at a waymark post along a track. Keep ahead, ignore side turnings; track ascends and passes another waymark post to reach the top of the hill.

4. Bear L and in a few yards at a waymark post by a silver birch tree, turn L (not ahead) along a surfaced track. Ignore all side turnings, eventually just before passing the derelict Blackwater Lodge on your L, note the Bronze Age tumulus on your R (unfortunately overgrown). Keep ahead with the Gibraltar Barracks boundary fence on your L, in ½ mile reach and carefully cross the busy Minley Road to return to start.

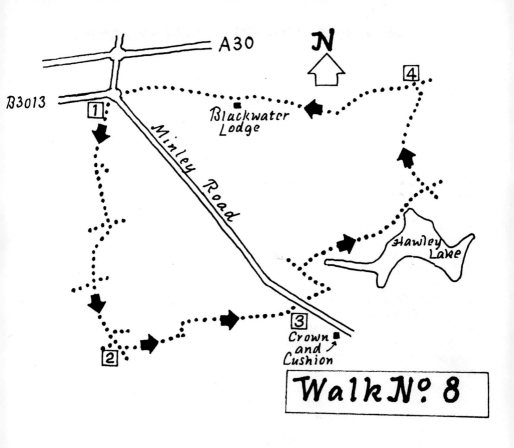

Walk Nº 8

Crown & Cushion

Minley Road   Telephone: 01252 545253

Open 12 noon to 11 pm (Monday to Saturday) and 10.30 pm Sunday

Carvery Lunch served Sunday to Friday,
Bar Snacks 12 noon to 2 pm and 6 to 9.30 pm

Large Patio Area overlooking Cricket Green

Traditional Country Inn with Mead Banqueting Hall

Walk No 9   FARLEY HILL & LOWER COMMON

[4½ miles - 2¼ hours]

1. Start from the Fox & Hounds*, Farley Hill. Cross Jouldings Lane and just beyond Brockendale, turn R at the footpath signpost along the enclosed path. At the fence, turn R along the bottom of the garden and then L along the enclosed path. Turn R over a stile and go along the RH field edge; shortly turn L at a footpath signpost and across the field aiming for a post and then go along the LH field edge. Cross the stile in the corner of the field, go ahead across the large field aiming for a large pylon.

2. Keep ahead to a stile and footbridge and follow the path through the wood. At the far side of the wood by a post at its corner, cross the field to its RH corner. Go along the RH edge of the next field, at the corner of the field by a white house, turn R along a track leading to a road via a track.

3. Turn R along the road and fork R passing Greenacres Farm signs. At the footpath signpost go ahead on a track, at the next footpath signpost by an iron gate, bear R over a stile and go along the track. Soon look out for a 3-fingered footpath signpost on your R, turn R over a stile [marked the Blackwater Valley Footpath] and across the field to a stile in its opposite LH corner. Cross this and a further stile and go along the LH field edge with the Blackwater River on your L. At the third stile, turn L at a footpath signpost along an enclosed path to pass Jouldings Farm and reach a road.

4. Cross the road to a stile and footpath signpost opposite. Go along the LH field edges by the river, crossing a stile and three footbridges to reach a road at Thatchers Ford. Cross the road and stile continuing by the riverside. [Do not cross the river footbridge] Shortly pass the confluence of the Blackwater and Whitewater Rivers. Keep ahead by the river and in due course at the overhead cables, turn R over a stile by a metal gate and along an enclosed path and over a stile to reach a road.

5. Turn R along the road and L along Sandpit Lane when the T-junction is reached. After 350 yards, look out for a footpath signpost on your L, ascend some steps and go along the LH field edge. At a waymark on a wooden sleeper post, bear R and descend across the field and continue along the road. At the T-junction, turn R and cross Church Road with care to a byway signpost opposite. Bear half L along the drive and track beside Victory Hall and Farley Hill Church. Turn R along Castle Road and L along Church Road to return to the Fox & Hounds.

* *Please ask the Landlords permission to use the car park.*

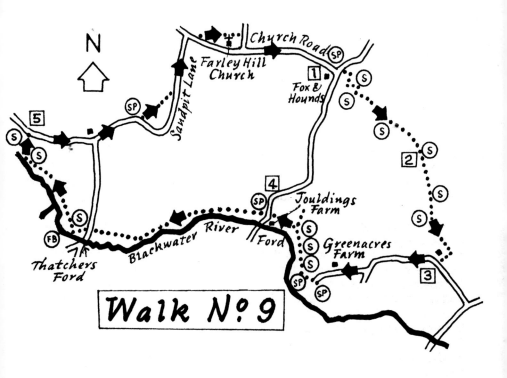

Walk Nº 9

Walk No 10   FINCHAMPSTEAD & BLACKWATER RIVER

[4½ miles, 2¼ hours]

1. Start from Finchampstead Church [or see end of paragraph 3]. Enter the churchyard and pass to the R of the church tower, descend on the path, through a kissing gate and along the enclosed path. In 100 yards at a 3-fingered signpost, turn R along an enclosed path; just beyond a signpost, turn L and then R. At a T-junction by white buildings, turn L and soon over a stile, along a drive to reach a road.

2. Cross the busy road with care, turn L [watch traffic] and just before the garage, turn R at a signpost, over a stile and along an enclosed path. At a 3-fingered signpost (with the Catherine of Aragon plaque) by the end of a road , turn R along a track. At another 3-fingered signpost keep ahead, soon cross a wooden footbridge. Shortly turn L through a kissing gate along a gravel path [Blackwater Valley Footpath] along the RH edge of a large field. In due course reach and carefully cross the busy road to a kissing gate opposite on your R.

3. Continue along the enclosed gravel path on the RH side of a large field. Turn L along the path that follows the Blackwater River. Pass but do not cross a gravel extraction bridge on your R. Eventually cross a small wooden footbridge [not over the Blackwater] and turn L along the RH of two enclosed tracks [the other one is a bridleway]. Pass Moor Green Lakes on your R, go over a wooden bridge and keep along the RH track. In due course reach a road.
NOTE The walk can be started from the car park there.

4. Turn L along the road and in 150 yards, turn R along Dell Road. Road winds and ascends onto the Finchampstead Ridges to reach and cross a busy road to a bridleway signpost opposite.

5. Go along the bridleway. Ignore the LH turn at the top of the hill [just before Wick Hill House] and keep ahead. The bridleway narrows at Tudor Cottage [on your L], the track descends and eventually passes through a wooden barrier on to a surfaced road. Keep ahead, shortly the road bears R, fork L on an earth track that soon ascends. At Silver Wood on your R, turn L at a signpost by a blue gate and in a few yards at Warren Crest Farm, fork R along a wide enclosed track. Go through a gap and keep ahead on an enclosed path, then through a kissing gate to reach a road.

6. Cross with care the busy road to the signpost and kissing gate opposite. Bear half L diagonally across the field to its opposite LH corner. Turn R up the road [watch traffic] and pass the Queens Oak pub and return to the Church.
NOTE There is a good footpath map between the pub and the church.

N

Walk Nº 10

Queens Oak
1

6

5

Finchampstead Ridges

2

B3016

3

4 Car Park

Moor Green Lakes

Blackwater River

Eversley Cross

Walk No 11   COVE BROOK & HAWLEY COMMON

[5½ miles, 2¾ hours]

1. Start from the car park by the bridge over Cove Brook near to Highfield Path. Go along Highfield Path, at the end of the road enter the enclosed path leading to Holly Road. Shortly turn L along a tarmac track, under the railway bridge and turn L along the path at the base of the embankment. At the Five Arch Bridge, turn R along the path on the RHS of Cove Brook.

2. Shortly cross West Heath Road and continue on the footpath opposite on the RHS of Cove Brook. Cross the footbridge over Cove Brook, turn R across a large grass area. Cross back over Cove Brook by the footbridge, turn L along a gravel path on the RHS of Cove Brook. Pass but do not cross another foot-bridge over Cove Brook and continue on the gravel path on the RHS of Cove Brook.

3. Cross a road and continue on the gravel path opposite. Pass but do not cross a further footbridge over Cove Brook and continue on the gravel brook-side footpath. Go under the M3 bridge and keep ahead to reach Hawley Lane.

4. Turn L along the footway and just before the roundabout, cross with great care Hawley Road. Turn L along the footway and shortly pass The New Inn. Keep ahead beyond Ashbury Drive and soon pass Fernhill Lane on your L. [The walk can be shortened by turning L up Fernhill Lane] Soon leave the busy Hawley Road and bear R on a tarmac track passing cottages and go along the old road. Go through a gap, keep on the old road that soon merges with Hawley Road. Go ahead on the footway to reach Hawley Lodge on your R.

5. With great care, cross the busy Hawley Road to the field gate opposite. Cross the metal stile, turn L on the path across the field [with a metal fence on your R] to cross another metal stile to reach Fernhill Lane. Turn R up Fernhill Lane [no footway for 700 yards]; ignore all side turnings and in due course descend to Fernhill Road.

6. Cross the road with great care, turn R on the footway up the hill and just beyond Abercorn House, turn L along Woodlands Walk. At Hawley Place Gardens, pass a wooden gate and keep ahead on a wide bridleway. Ignore all side turnings and in just over ½ mile, fork R off the track to pass Hawley Lake on your R. Go ahead on a tarmac road crossing a brick parapet bridge over the outlet stream of Hawley Lake. Shortly fork L at a Y-junction and on reaching a wooden fence on your L, go through a barrier and along a wide gravel meandering path [buildings on your R]. Turn L along a concrete road to reach Sandy Lane.

7. Cross the road with care to The Potteries opposite; shortly turn R on a path through trees and pass under the M3 via a narrow bridge. Go ahead along Woodlands Road to reach and carefully cross Minley Road. Turn L along the footway and enter St Johns churchyard. Leave it by the lychgate and take the enclosed church path opposite.

8. Turn R along Minley Road and go clockwise past the roundabout. Just before the railway bridge, turn L along the footpath behind the houses. Go over the Five Arch Bridge and soon turn R under the railway bridge and R again along Holly Road and Highfield Path to return to the start.

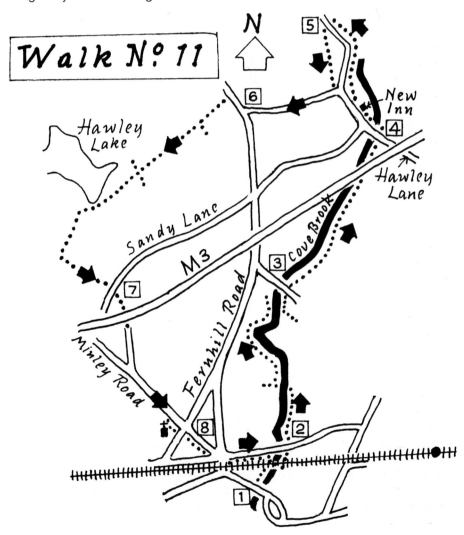

Walk No 12   BLACKWATER RIVER & BASINGSTOKE CANAL

[5 miles, 2½ hours]

1. Start from Carrington Recreation car park, Ash Vale. [Note car park closes at dusk]. Go along the tarmac drive (with the large green on your L), past the red & white barrier, turn L and carefully cross Lysons Avenue. Turn R into the side road and over North Camp Station level crossing. Keep ahead on the road and in a few yards at a Blackwater Valley Path signpost, turn R across the road and under a bridge (beside Blackwater River)

2. Cross over Lynchford Lane and soon turn R at a Blackwater Valley Path North signpost. Go along a gravel path beside the busy Blackwater Valley Road, pass a gasometer on your R, over a railway bridge and descend on a path that passes under the road (beside the Blackwater River). Shortly cross a footbridge over the Blackwater River and go through Gerrys Copse. Recross the river on a footbridge, turn L along the track and soon fork L on a footpath. Cross another footbridge over the river and in due course go up a slope to Coleford Bridge Road.

3. Turn R at a Blackwater Valley Path North signpost, over the bridge, turn R down some steps and turn R along a broad track going under the bridge. Pass the Quays sign on your R, fork R down a path to the R of a metal gate and follow the path beside the Blackwater River. Cross a footbridge and turn R along the track, go under the railway bridge, pass under a concrete bridge and turn R over another footbridge. Do NOT turn L through a gate along the Blackwater Valley Path, but go ahead on an enclosed bridleway, The Hatches, that passes between lakes. Carefully go over the railway level crossing to reach the road.

4. Go ahead on The Hatches, turn R at Cross Lane and follow The Hatches to pass Frimley Green on your L (Rose & Thistle opposite). Cross Sturt Road with care, turn R and then under the railway bridge. Pass St Andrews Church and turn L into Frimley Lodge Park. [NOTE the walk can be started from here] Keep along the track with the car park on your L. Pass on your R a signpost to the Pavilion and Canal North. Follow the track to the R of the Pavilion with a sports field on your R. At the crossing of a tarmac road, turn L and arrive at the Frimley Lodge Park Miniature Railway wooden shed. Turn L and reach the Basingstoke Canal towpath.

5. Turn R along the towpath and in due course pass the Basingstoke Canal Centre, under Mytchett Place Road bridge and next Mytchett Lake Road bridge to pass Mytchett Lake. Soon pass under the railway bridge and turn R off the towpath down a short track to reach the road. Turn L along Frimley Road and in 250 yards carefully cross the road and turn R into Carrington Lane to return to the start.

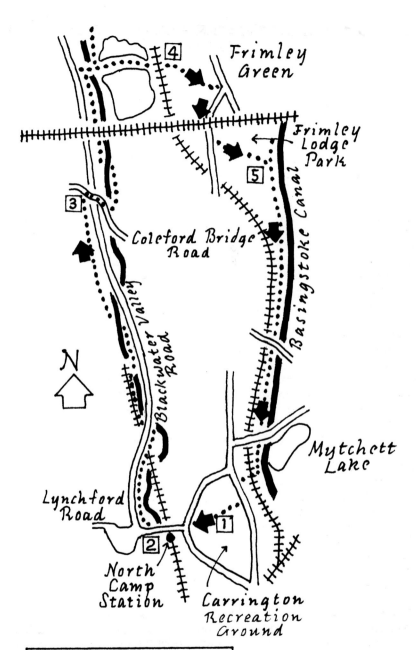

Frimley
Green

Frimley
Lodge
Park

Basingstoke Canal

Coleford Bridge
Road

N

Blackwater Valley
Road

Mytchett
Lake

Lynchford
Road

Carrington
Recreation
Ground

North
Camp
Station

Walk Nº 12

POINTS OF INTEREST

Eversley

Castle Bottom is close to the site of former cottages on Eversley Common, but little trace of them remains. It is a surprisingly isolated hollow of ancient heathland that is now a Nature Reserve and is close to Blackbushe Airfield. Traces of a low round tumulus were said to be obliterated by wartime airfield works. It was on the main dyke boundary of Crondall Manor confirmed by King Edgar in 975. A bank along the parish boundary to the present A30 was made by the Militia encamped locally in 1803. [Walk No 2]

The Church of Blessed Mary the Virgin There was a church on the site by 1294. The chancel was built about 1500; in 1724 the whole church, west of the chancel screen, was re-built by John James. The tower was completed in 1736. In 1876 the church was 'restored as a memorial to Charles Kingsley, rector from 1844 until his death in 1875. He was a social reformer, naturalist, author of The Water-Babies, but probably most importantly a simple, well-loved, parish priest. He was buried beside the avenue of yews he planted in the churchyard. [Walk Nos 1, 2 & 3]

Cross Green Eversleys ancient origins are suggested by the village sign erected on the green commemorating Queen Elizabeths Silver Jubilee in 1975. Eversleys name may be derived from *Efor Leigh* or field of the wild boar. It is one of the few remaining records of the existence of wild boars in England. The cricket ground on the green is the venue of an annual benefit match with Hampshire. Close to the pond are the remains of a unusual spigot mortar, erected during of the 1940 defence works. [Walk No 3]

Firgrove Manor Wadham Wyndham prospered in the service of the South Sea Company and this, together with a dowry of £ 8000 on marrying his cousin Catherine, enabled him early in the 18th century to build Firgrove Manor - possibly by John James. It may occupy the site of an earlier building or monastery. The Wyndhams were a Saxon family of nobility from Norfolk. They were one of the two leading families in Yateley and strong supporters of the Jacobites in southern England. Wadham Wyndham was a well-known amateur coachman.

[Walk Nos 2 & 3]

New Mill dates from 1577 when it replaced an earlier mill destroyed by fire. The Domesday Book records two mills in the vicinity. For over three hundred years New Mill was owned by the St John family who rented it to the Spencers. A later tenant, Mr Westcott, added the lock bridge and started a saw mill. Local farmers brought corn to the mill for grinding until early in the 20th century. New Mill is a listed building and has been a restaurant since 1972. The water wheel and corn grinding equipment are still in working order.

[Walk No 1]

Warbrook House was built in 1724 by the architect John James for himself. Despite recent additions, the period building has survived virtually intact. The grounds were laid out using the principles of Dezallier d'Argentville; James translated the French Treatise. The West front of Warbrook House has a breath-taking view down the tree-lined canal which exemplifies his mastery of landscaping. James was born in 1672 at Stratfield Turgis, educated at Basingstoke and apprenticed to Matthew Bankes, the Kings Carpenter. He became an architect and, as a colleage of Christopher Wren, was involved in the completion of St Pauls Cathedral where he was surveyor to the fabric. He designed many other buildings in London after the Great Fire in 1666 and also a number of buildings in Hampshire. His achievements are recorded on a memorial tablet in Eversley Church. [Walk No 1] **The Welsh Drive** is an old drovers road used to take cattle from Wales and the West Country to London. This stopped when the railways developed. An annual fair was held on 8 November at Blackwater. The Welsh Drive passes close to Cudbury Clump a Bronze Age burial barrow. [Walk Nos 1 & 2]

Finchampstead

Catherine of Aragon In 1501 Prince Arthur, eldest son of Henry VII, started out from Windsor Castle to meet his fiancee Catherine of Aragon. He was met at Finchampstead by her guardians. The meeting spot is marked by a plaque. Against royal Spanish custom, Prince Henry rode on to meet her at Dogmersfield. A dance was held there in the evening. [Walk Nos 5 & 10]

Finchampstead Ridges is National Trust property and provides a fine viewpoint across the Blackwater Valley and parts of Berkshire, Hampshire and Surrey. Just to the north, the London to Silchester Roman Road called the Devils Highway crosses Simons Wood. Wellingtonia Avenue is an outstanding half-mile avenue of hundred Sequoia trees, planted in 1863 in memory of the Duke of Wellington. [Walk Nos 6 & 10]

Moor Green Lakes are a nature reserve restored from former gravel pits. Habitats have been created for a wide variety of birds which can be seen from the Blackwater Valley Footpath. [Walks Nos 6 & 10]

Parish Church of St James retains the walls of the original church built about the time of the Norman Conquest. The Normans elaborated the simple Saxon church to its more or less present form in about 1150. The font is the original - credited 1030. About 1375 a small chapel was added on the north side removing part of the Norman wall. The chapel was extended about 1475 and a corner entrance constructed in 1590. The red brick tower built in 1720 has six bells dating from 1792. A list of rectors from 1299 is in the 19th century porch. [Walk Nos 5 & 10]

Hawley

Crown & Cushion has associations with Colonel Thomas Blood who lived at Minley Warren. In 1671 he nearly succeeded in stealing the Crown Jewels from the Tower of London. Although he escaped, he was later arrested whilst imbibing in the Crown & Cushion. This was commemorated by a topiary in front of the pub cut in the shape of a crown on a cushion, sadly no longer trimmed. Blood was granted a Royal Pardon and an estate in Ireland worth £ 500 a year. Who said crime does not pay! [Walk No 8]

Hawley Lake in Hawley Common is a popular walking, sailing and fishing area. The Common was part of the Minley Manor grounds owned by the Currie family, local benefactors who gave ground for the cricket pavilion by Hawley Green and later for the Hawley War Memorial Hall. The lake and surrounding common are now used by the Royal Engineers as a training area and walkers should keep to the paths. [Walk Nos 8 & 11]

Minley Manor was rebuilt in 1858-60 for Raikes Currie a London Banker and MP for Northampton. The architect was Henry Clutton and the design was said to be inspired by the Chateau de Blois. The Manor was enlarged later and remained with the Currie family until it was purchased by the War Office in 1936. Since 1971 it has been used by the Royal Engineers from the adjacent Gibraltar Barracks. [Walk No 8]

Sandhurst

Ambarrow Court was built in 1885 for Colonel Harvey from designs by the architect F Ravenscroft; it was surrounded by over 21 acres of woodland. On his widows death, it was offered for sale in 1932 by Messrs Nicholas of Reading for use as a school, nursing home or institution. In Autumn 1940 it was requisitioned as an outstation of Radio Department, Royal Aircraft Establishment following the bombing of RAE Farnborough in August 1940. The house was then empty, but it contained much German literature which lends credence to the rumours that it had been used for the interrogation of enemy agents. After it was relinquished by the RAE in 1969, it became derelict and the house was demolished. Fortunately the weather-cock has been preserved on a building in the RAE. The grounds, once a secret garden, are now open to the public as is adjacent Ambarrow Hill.

[Walk No6]

Yateley

Blackbushe airfield was built on common land in the Second World War and was known as RAF Hartford Bridge. It was crossed by the Welsh Drive and the road over the common to Vigo Lane which has never been re-opened. One runway crossed the A30 and traffic was diverted onto the Fleet Road. The airfield was first used by Aerodynamics Flight, Royal Aircraft Establishment testing gliders later used at D-Day. A variety of operational squadrons used the airfield including: RCAF Tomahawks, RAF photographic reconnaissance Spitfires, RAF and Free French Boston bombers and Polish Mosquitos. The airfield had FIDO - a fog dispersal system. There is a memorial plaque at the airfield honouring aircrew lost in action. [Walk No 7]

St Peters Parish Church is built on the site of a Saxon church said to have been burnt down about 750. The earliest record of the church is in the Domesday Book 1080. There is a roll of incumbents back to 1226. The north wall from behind the wooden font to the organ is Saxon and was extended to its present length in about 1100. The chancel was completed about 1220 and the wooden tower about 1500. The church was burnt down in 1979 leaving only the walls, charred timbers of the tower and cracked bells - the oldest cast in 1557. The church was re-built by 1981. The chancel became the chapel and contains the 13th century font; the 1600 clock was restored. [Walk No 7]

Yateley Common Country Park is one of the few remaining heathlands in North East Hampshire. It was originally cleared of forest in the Bronze Age for crops and livestock. The poor soil was soon exhausted and colonised by plants such as heather and gorse. For hundreds of years it was kept open by commoners cutting fuel and turf and by continuous grazing. As this declined, birch and pine invaded the Common. This has been reversed by the Country Park Rangers careful management. Stroud Pond was recorded in the Domesday Book as a fish pond; stakes to prevent poaching have been traced. Wyndhams Pool is named after a local family. [Walk No 4]

Blackwater Valley Footpath

Blackwater River has its source in Rowhill Nature Reserve between Aldershot and Farnham. The river forms the county boundaries between Hampshire, Surrey and Berkshire. A continuous footpath follows the course of Blackwater River from its source to its confluence with the River Loddon. Many of the circular walks described in this book follow sections of the Blackwater Valley Footpath or give a vistas across the Blackwater Valley. There is also a footpath beside Cove Brook, a tributary of the Blackwater, which unfortunately does not connect with it.

Thatchers Ford is where the Roman Road (known as the Devils Highway) crossed the Blackwater River. [Walk No 9]